POLES APART

EXPLORING ANTARCTICA

Illustrated by Oliver Averill

FRANKLIN WATTS
LONDON • SYDNEY

First published in Great Britain in 2025
by Hodder & Stoughton

Copyright © Hodder & Stoughton Limited, 2025

All rights reserved.

Authors: Julia Adams, Anita Ganeri, Sonya Newland, Louise Spilsbury

Editors: Julia Adams and Victoria Brooker
Designer: Peter Scoulding

HB ISBN: 978 1 4451 9156 0
PB ISBN: 978 1 4451 9158 4
EBK ISBN: 978 1 5263 9157 7

Printed in Dubai

Franklin Watts
An imprint of
Hachette Children's Group
Part of Hodder & Stoughton
Carmelite House
50 Victoria Embankment
London EC4Y 0DZ

An Hachette UK Company
www.hachette.co.uk
www.hachettechildrens.co.uk

The authorised representative in the EEA is Hachette Ireland, 8 Castlecourt Centre, Dublin 15, D15 XTP3, Ireland
(email: info@hbgi.ie)

CONTENTS

The Polar Regions   4
Icy Desert   6
Snow and Ice   8
Frozen Ocean   10
Life in Cold Water   12
Winter   14
Southern Lights   16
Diamond Dust   18
Spring   20
Antarctic Food Web   22
Antarctic Plants   24
Giants of the Deep   26
Seals   28
Penguin Paradise   30
Birds   32
Exploring Antarctica   34
Who Lives on Antarctica?   36
Cold Science   38
Human Impact   40
Under Threat   42
The Future   44
Glossary   46
Further information   47
Index   48

THE POLAR REGIONS

LYING AT BOTH ENDS OF THE EARTH, the two polar regions – the Arctic and Antarctic – make up about 8 per cent of the world's surface. Covered in vast expanses of ice and snow, and battered by gale-force winds, the poles are among the Earth's coldest, most isolated and hostile habitats.

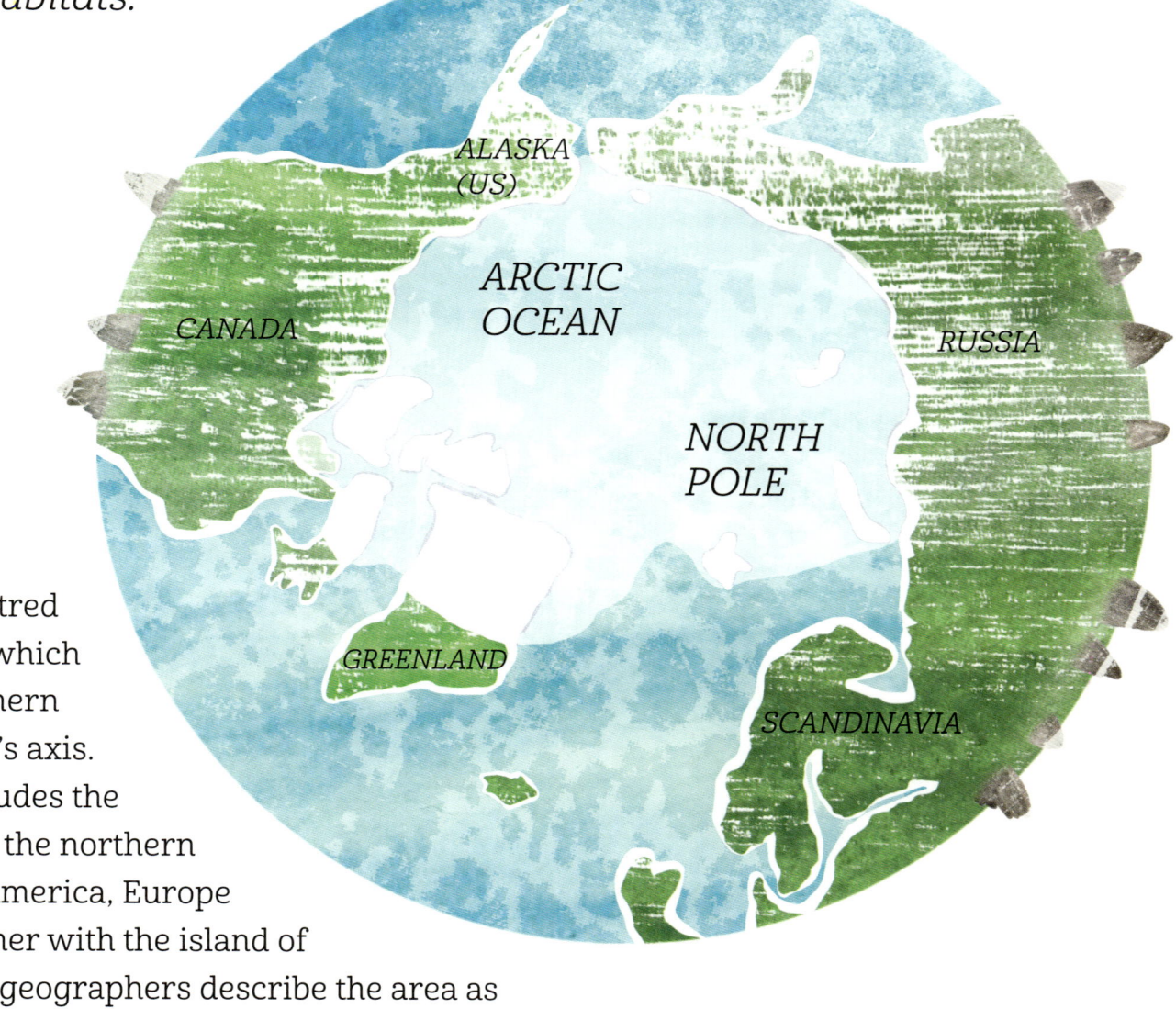

The **ARCTIC** is centred on the North Pole which marks the northern end of the Earth's axis. The region includes the Arctic Ocean and the northern parts of North America, Europe and Asia, together with the island of Greenland. Some geographers describe the area as the Arctic Circle, an imaginary line drawn around the northernmost part of the Earth.

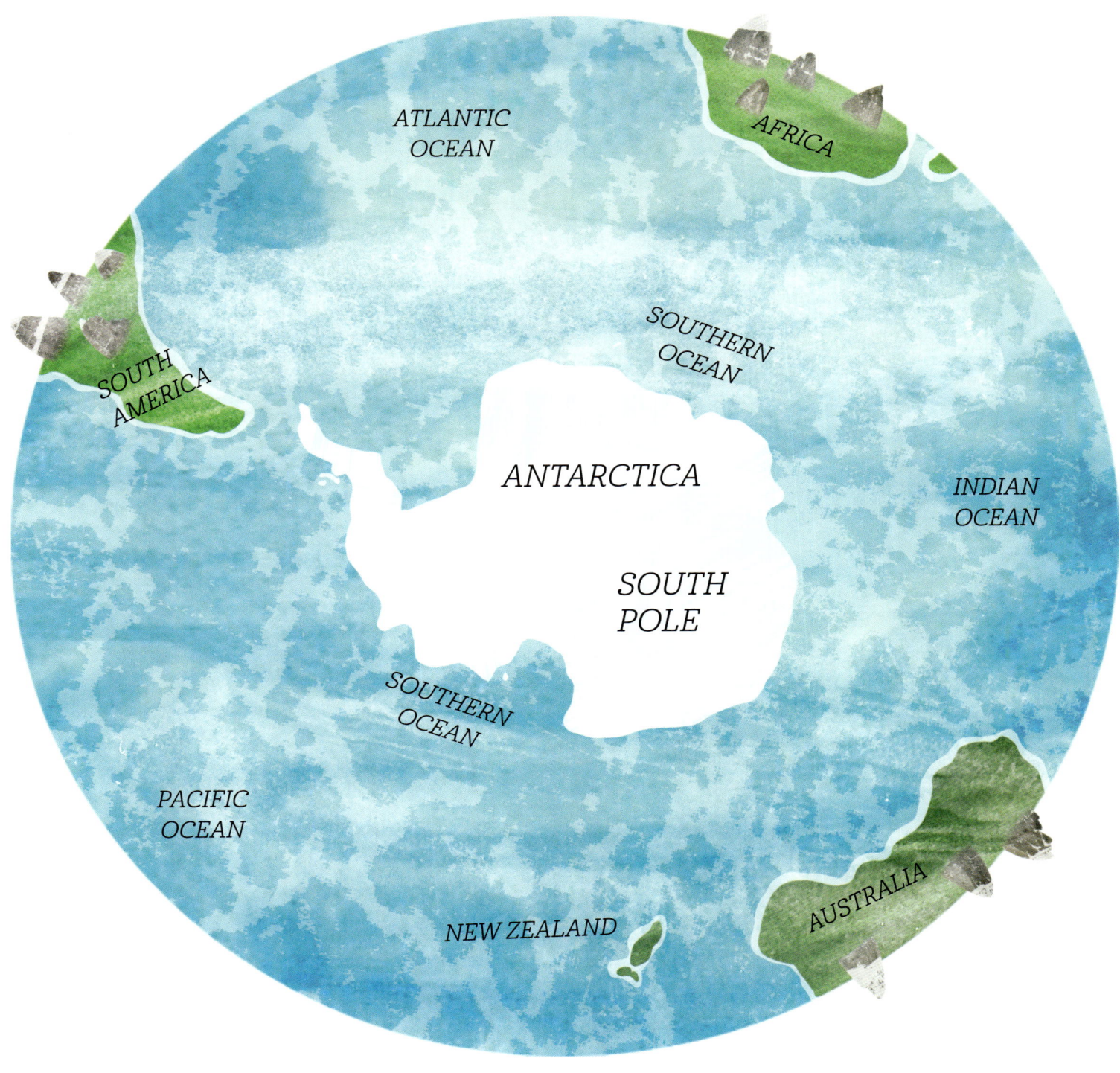

The name **ANTARCTIC** is used to describe the region around the South Pole, which marks the southern end of Earth's axis. The region includes the continent of Antarctica and the sea around it, which is called the Southern Ocean.

ICY DESERT

THE ANTARCTIC is a frozen continent surrounded by sea, with the South Pole roughly in the middle of it. The continent of Antarctica covers about 14 million sq km, as big as the USA and Mexico combined.

About 98 per cent of Antarctica is capped by ice. The vast covering of ice also helps to keep Antarctica cold. Instead of soaking up the Sun's rays, the white ice reflects most of the heat back into space. This is called the **ALBEDO EFFECT**: light colours reflect heat away, while dark colours absorb heat.

Buried beneath the ice are mountains and volcanoes, including the active volcano **MOUNT EREBUS**. At its summit, peaking above the ice, is an active lava lake.

Antarctica counts as a **DESERT** because it receives only 150 mm of rain or snow each year. Only very few plants are able to grow in these conditions, so nearly all Antarctic animals rely on the ocean for food.

SNOW AND ICE

THE LANDSCAPE OF ANTARCTICA *is dominated by ice. Because of the bitter cold, any snow that falls on the land rarely melts, but settles in layers. The weight of each new layer presses down on the layers beneath, packing them down until they turn into ice.*

Antarctica is covered by the largest single mass of ice on Earth, which contains about 90 per cent of the world's fresh water. The ice is so heavy that the underlying land has sunk below sea level beneath its weight.

At its thickest, the ice reaches almost 5,000 m and is millions of years old. Under the force of gravity, ice from the centre of the ice sheets flows towards the coast in frozen rivers called **GLACIERS**. In places, these float out to sea as massive ice shelves.

Each year, thousands of chunks of ice break off the glaciers and ice sheets to form **ICEBERGS**. They vary in size from small 'growlers' the size of pianos, to towering icebergs as tall as ten-storey buildings.

FROZEN OCEAN

WHEN THE SEA FREEZES, it forms a type of salty ice, called sea ice. The sea around Antarctica is frozen over for most of the year.

The Antarctic sea ice reaches its greatest extent in September, when it covers up to 20 million sq km of the **SOUTHERN OCEAN**, more than doubling the size of the Antarctic. The ice is about 1 to 2 m thick. Nearly all the sea ice melts in summer.

The wind and waves keep sea ice constantly on the move. They also break it up to form pack ice. Individual pieces of pack ice are called **FLOES**, which can be more than 10 km across. Pack ice is so heavy and hard, it can tear a ship's hull.

As the ice drifts, the floes sometimes collide, forming great mounds of ice, called **PRESSURE RIDGES**. Other times, cracks and channels, called leads, form. These can speed up the spring melt and provide access to the ocean for land animals, such as penguins.

LIFE IN COLD WATER

FOR ANIMALS THAT LIVE in the polar oceans, keeping warm is vital. An animal's cells contain water. If this freezes, it stops the cells from working properly, damages tissues and causes death.

Many of the invertebrates that live on the bottom of the Southern Ocean grow and move very slowly to save energy. Some of these creatures reach an unusually large size.

A relative of the common woodlouse, **GLYPTONOTUS** is a crustacean that can grow up to 20 cm long. That's over ten times as long as an ordinary woodlouse.

Mackerel icefish (up to 44 cm long)

Glyptonotus (up to 20 cm long)

Giant sea spider (up to 30 cm diameter)

Fish are more at risk than **INVERTEBRATES**. Seawater freezes at about −1.8°C, while a fish's body fluids and blood freeze at higher temperatures. Many Antarctic fish have a chemical, like anti-freeze, in their blood, which lowers their freezing point to a safer −2.5°C.

Beneath the pack ice, the sea stays unfrozen all year round and the temperature does not change much. **KRILL** and other invertebrates that live in the sea are therefore protected from freezing – unless they get trapped in the ice.

Anasterias antarctica starfish (up to 8 cm across)

White-blooded icefish (up to 49 cm long)

WINTER

THE ANTARCTIC WINTER lasts from March to October. For most of winter, the Sun does not rise, plunging the South Pole into months of darkness. Further away from the South Pole, the sky is in constant twilight.

Once the temperatures start sinking, sea ice builds up and gradually blocks off access to the ocean. Many mammals and birds who rely on the ocean as a source of food migrate to **WARMER AREAS** during the winter months.

Some areas of the ocean remain ice-free, due to winds and water currents that keep sea ice from forming here. These areas are called **POLYNYAS**, and they are an oasis for overwintering animals, such as penguins and seals.

Antarctic winter is extremely cold, with an average temperature of –60°C. Sometimes temperatures can even drop below –80°C. With wind speeds of up to 300 km per hour, the felt temperature can be even colder. This is called the **WINDCHILL FACTOR**.

SOUTHERN LIGHTS

THE LOCATION OF ANTARCTICA makes it the perfect place to witness the famous aurora australis, or southern lights. Auroras look like ribbons of light dancing across the sky. They occur all year round but can only be seen when the sky is dark.

AURORA colours range from glowing greens and yellows to neon pinks, purples and blues.

Auroras occur close to the North and South Poles. Here, tiny particles from the Sun interact with Earth's **MAGNETIC FIELD**. They enter Earth's atmosphere and collide with its gases. These impacts produce tiny flashes that can be seen as bright colours glowing in the night sky.

DIAMOND DUST

WHEN THE TEMPERATURES dip below −10°C, any tiny water droplets in the air start to freeze and form ice crystals. These crystals are so small that they often remain suspended in the air for a while, sometimes even forming clouds higher up in the sky.

In Antarctica, these **TINY CRYSTALS** are present in the air most days of the year. During the summer, they glitter and sparkle in the sunlight, which is why they are often described as 'diamond dust'.

Depending on how the ice crystals reflect the sunlight, this sometimes creates a ring, or halo, around the Sun. Often this halo is white, but sometimes it can show in colours such as yellow or red.

Diamond dust can also create the illusion of '**SUN DOGS**' – one or two glowing spots that appear either side of the Sun. These spots can look a little like a rainbow, running from red on the side closest to the Sun, to blue on the far side of the Sun.

SPRING

IN OCTOBER, DAYLIGHT STARTS returning to Antarctica and, with it, warmer temperatures. Once the Sun rises over Antarctica, it remains in the sky and only sets again at the beginning of winter.

As spring arrives, the sea ice melts, and more and more animals arrive from their migrations in search of food. The loss of ice cover allows sunlight to reach tiny plants in the ocean, called **PHYTOPLANKTON**. The energy from the Sun helps them grow, and provides food for the rest of the Antarctic food web (see pages 22–23).

Large cracks, called **LEADS**, appear in the melting sea ice. These can be hundreds of metres wide. They offer penguins, seals and whales fresh hunting grounds, as well as pathways through the icy sea. As leads spread and grow, they help quicken the ice melt.

ANTARCTIC FOOD WEB

THE ANTARCTIC FOOD WEB BEGINS in the waters of the Southern Ocean. Every polar creature depends on phytoplankton, which are eaten by animal plankton, including krill. Krill form the main diet of many different Antarctic animals and, without it, the food web would collapse.

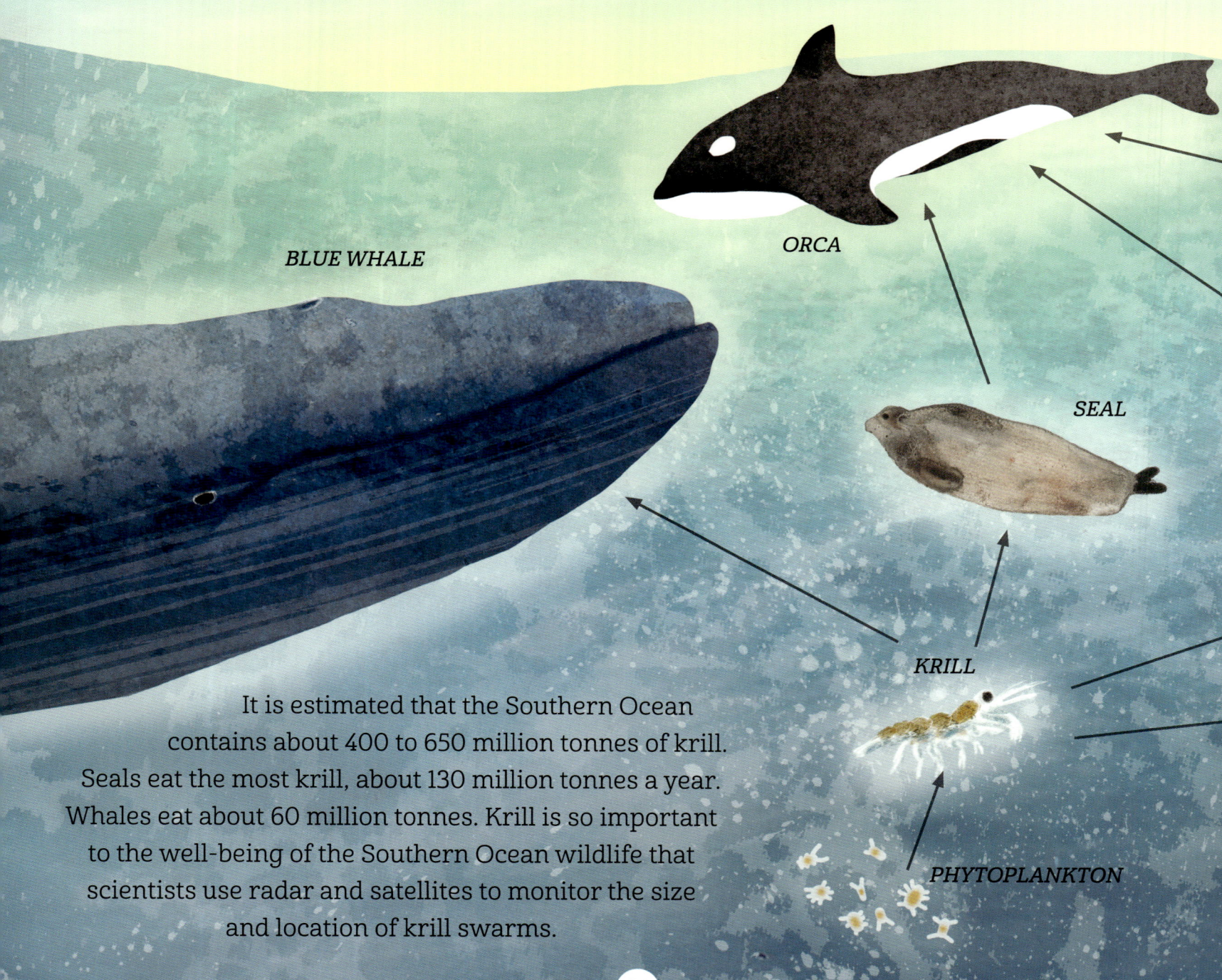

BLUE WHALE

ORCA

SEAL

KRILL

PHYTOPLANKTON

It is estimated that the Southern Ocean contains about 400 to 650 million tonnes of krill. Seals eat the most krill, about 130 million tonnes a year. Whales eat about 60 million tonnes. Krill is so important to the well-being of the Southern Ocean wildlife that scientists use radar and satellites to monitor the size and location of krill swarms.

ANTARCTIC PLANTS

ANTARCTICA'S EXTREME CONDITIONS mean that only the hardiest plants can live on land. Just two species of flowering plant survive on the Antarctic Peninsula. But over 400 species of lichen have been found in the few ice-free patches of rocks or ground.

LICHEN grow very slowly, since there may be only a few days in the year when conditions are suitable for growth. It can take a lichen more than 100 years to cover a patch of rock the size of a postage stamp. Some lichens can survive for over 2,000 years.

During the short summer, **MOSSES** carpet rocks along the shore. In turn, the moss carpets provide habitats for the two flowering plants that live in Antarctica – pearlwort and Antarctic hairgrass. The moss is also home to tiny invertebrates, less than 6 mm long, that use it as a food source.

The Antarctic ice sheet itself is almost bare, although some types of **ALGAE** grow on the snowfields near the coast. The algae feed on penguin poo and contain pigment that colours the snow – green in the spring and pink in autumn. Scientists sometimes call this 'watermelon snow'.

GIANTS OF THE DEEP

WHALES OF THE SOUTHERN OCEAN include blue, humpback, southern right, fin, sei and minke whales. They migrate long distances every year, feeding in the polar seas during the summer months, and heading to tropical waters in the north to breed in the winter.

The **southern right whale** can be recognised by its behaviour – it leaps out of the water (breach), slaps the water's surface with its flippers and smacks its flukes onto the water.

In order to catch krill, **humpback whales** dive downwards, releasing huge amounts of bubbles that form tall columns around swarms of krill. These 'bubble nets' trap the krill, making it easy for the whales to scoop them up.

At over 10 m in length, **blue whales** are the largest animals on Earth. They can eat about 16,000 kg of krill in one day.

When the **sei whale** dives, it doesn't arch its back and lift its tail (flukes) out of the water, like other whales. Instead, its whole body just sinks down.

The smallest of the Antarctic whales, the **minke whale** is also a very fast swimmer. It is hunted by some groups of orca, but often manages to outswim them.

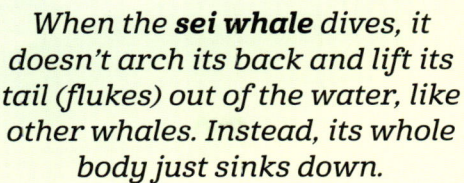

The **fin whale** can grow to be around 25 m long, and is named after the fin on its back. Besides krill, fin whales also feed on fish and squid.

SEALS

SEALS ARE WELL SUITED for life in the polar seas. They have streamlined bodies and paddle-like flippers for swimming, and thick layers of fat under their skin for warmth.

The **WEDDELL SEAL** lives farther south than any other mammal in the world. In summer, the seal breeds on the sea ice and islands around Antarctica. It spends the winter under the ice, searching for fish and squid to eat. It gnaws breathing holes in the ice with its large teeth.

SOUTHERN ELEPHANT SEALS are some of the largest seals in the world. The males can grow up to 6 m long. These seals spend their winters close to pack ice in the Southern Ocean, diving for fish and squid. In the summer, they visit the beaches of Antarctic islands to give birth and raise their pups.

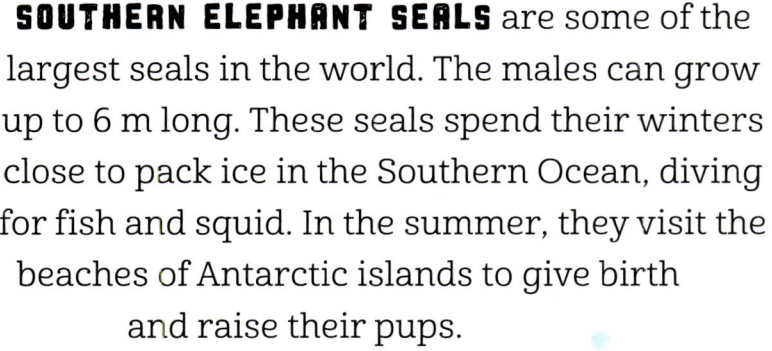

When penguins dive into the ocean to catch fish, they risk becoming prey themselves. **LEOPARD SEALS** often lurk under sea ice, ready to pounce on penguins and even small seals. These ferocious hunters are often born on pack ice and remain in the Southern Ocean all year.

PENGUIN PARADISE

THERE ARE 18 SPECIES OF PENGUIN, of which nine live in and around Antarctica. But only one species breeds during the extremely cold winter months of the icy continent.

PENGUINS are adapted to their icy habitat in a number of ways. Their feathers are short and tightly packed, and they have a thick layer of fat to protect them from the cold. They don't move easily on land, but they can move quickly through the water.

While most birds leave the Antarctic in autumn and head for warmer places, hardy **EMPEROR PENGUINS** remain and breed on the ice in mid-winter. The female lays a single egg, then spends the winter at sea. Meanwhile, the male incubates the egg on his feet, tucked under a warm flap of skin.

For the next two months, in temperatures below −40°C and in strong winds, he and thousands of other males hardly move, huddling tightly together for warmth. By the time the female returns to feed the chick, the male has lost half his body weight. Then it is his turn to go out to sea to feed.

BIRDS

POLAR BIRDS ARE WELL PROTECTED against the cold, with dense feathers and thick layers of fat under their skins. Despite these adaptations, the winters are too harsh for flying birds. In summer, however, they visit to feed and even nest.

Each year, the **ARCTIC TERN** flies non-stop for eight months and covers 40,000 km to spend summer at either end of the Earth. During the Arctic summer, it breeds around the shores of the Arctic Ocean. Then it flies south to Antarctica to take advantage of the rich summer food supplies.

Wandering **ALBATROSSES** only come ashore in the summer to breed on Antarctic islands. They spend the rest of their lives in flight. Their 3.5-m wingspan allows them to soar and glide over the Southern Ocean as they search for fish and squid. They can stay in the air for months on end, only briefly landing on the water to feed.

Scientists sometimes describe **SOUTHERN SKUAS** as the pirates of the skies, as they steal other seabirds' prey. Southern skuas breed in Antarctica during the summer, and overwinter in Australia.

EXPLORING ANTARCTICA

ANTARCTICA IS EXTREMELY REMOTE and ringed by the planet's stormiest seas, so for centuries, people could only guess that any land might be there. On maps, it was marked as 'unknown southern land'.

The first people to discover Antarctica were whale- and seal-hunters. An American sealer, **JOHN DAVIS**, may have made the first known landing in 1821. Two years later, a ship, captained by British sealer James Weddell, sailed into the sea that now carries his name.

At the turn of the 20th century, expeditions were launched to reach the South Pole, whatever the cost. In 1911, the Norwegian **ROALD AMUNDSEN** led the first successful expedition.

In 1914, English-Irish explorer **ERNEST SHACKLETON** set sail with a crew to cross the Antarctic continent via the South Pole. After their ship, *Endurance*, got crushed in pack ice, the crew had to fight for their survival. They managed to cross the Southern Ocean and survive on a remote island until they were all rescued about 10 months later.

WHO LIVES ON ANTARCTICA?

TO THIS DAY, THE CONDITIONS in Antarctica mean that no humans live there permanently. However, many scientists and tourists visit the continent for short periods of time.

Scientists from all over the world visit Antarctica and stay for weeks or months, mainly during the summer. They examine wildlife and how animals thrive in this natural freezer. They also research how **CLIMATE CHANGE** is affecting this region.

Every summer, **THOUSANDS OF TOURISTS** visit Antarctica to enjoy the breathtaking scenery and unique wildlife. Most arrive on cruise ships that offer guided daytrips to the shores of the icy continent. Even though the rules are strict, tourists can threaten the fragile environment by leaving litter and disturbing wildlife.

No one owns Antarctica, but, in 1959, 12 countries signed a document called the **ANTARCTIC TREATY**, aimed at safeguarding Antarctica for the future. Today, 58 countries have signed up, promising to protect the region against severe environmental damage and to only use it for peaceful purposes.

COLD SCIENCE

SCIENTISTS carrying out research in Antarctica need specially built research stations. These are buildings in which they can live and work in extreme temperatures.

Around **ANTARCTICA** there are large, permanent stations. All polar labs are made from materials specially brought here because there are no trees to supply wood for building. Bases are often built on legs to keep the floors off the freezing, icy ground and to stop snow piling up in front of doors, trapping researchers inside.

HALLEY VI is a research station located on an ice shelf that observes the weather and climate around the South Pole. Its eight connected cabins sit on top of extendable stilts, each fitted with skis. If the weather or ice conditions become dangerous, the entire station can be towed to a new site.

The **ROTHERA RESEARCH STATION** is a collection of large buildings with research facilities including a seawater aquarium, where Antarctic marine life is studied. There is a runway and a hangar for aeroplanes and a wharf for ships to dock. There are bulk fuel storage tanks and a garage where vehicles are stored and repaired.

HUMAN IMPACT

ANTARCTICA IS ONE OF the last truly wild places on Earth. It is home to an amazing range of wildlife. It is also a fragile ecosystem, so scientists try to have zero impact on the environment while they work there.

Until the late 20th century, scientists dumped waste on the ice or in the sea. There are still piles of waste, such as old fuel drums. In some areas, whole affected areas of the ocean are now toxic. This type of pollution **DAMAGES WILDLIFE** and habitats. Today, waste is disposed of more carefully.

Labs have sewage **TREATMENT PLANTS** that clean wastewater from toilets and sinks so it can be discharged safely into the sea. Other waste is packed up and removed by ship or burned in an incinerator. Any remaining ash is then removed by ship.

Research stations need electricity to power heaters, cookers, computers and other equipment. One way of producing electricity is with a generator, but this causes pollution and releases carbon dioxide into the atmosphere. To avoid this, some research labs have started using **SOLAR ENERGY** systems, which generate electricity using the abundant summer sunlight.

The Earth is getting warmer because of the **GREENHOUSE EFFECT**. Burning fossil fuels, such as oil, gas and coal, to generate energy is raising the amount of carbon dioxide in the atmosphere. Small amounts of carbon dioxide occur naturally and play a vital role in trapping the Sun's heat. But as the amount of this gas is increasing, the Earth is heating up.

UNDER THREAT

ANTARCTICA IS UNDER THREAT from human-caused climate change. This is a process that is changing the Earth's weather patterns and causing the planet's average temperatures to rise.

Already, Antarctic ice shelves are shrinking and breaking up. Many glaciers have started to **MELT AND RETREAT**. As more ice melts, the sea levels are rising, which is affecting low-lying coastal communities around the world.

If the Antarctic ice continues to melt, many of its habitats will be lost, with terrible consequences for the continent's wildlife. Some animals are already being affected by the changing landscape. Emperor penguins, who breed on sea ice, now struggle to find safe **BREEDING GROUNDS** that won't melt early, endangering their young chicks.

THE FUTURE

ANTARCTICA IS ALREADY *being affected by environmental threats, but many organisations and governments are working hard to protect this unique habitat. Their efforts are making a difference and could help secure Antarctica's future.*

In 2002, Australia established a fully protected marine reserve in its Antarctic waters. The reserve covers an area about one-and-a-half times the size of Switzerland and includes a group of remote islands that are home to several **THREATENED SPECIES**. To safeguard these animals and their habitat, the reserve strictly limits human activity.

Antarctic scientists are working on new recycling systems, as well as removing existing waste pollution that has been damaging the landscape for decades (see pages 40–41). The **PRINCESS ELIZABETH RESEARCH STATION** has even managed to become a zero-emissions facility, powered by nine wind turbines and 284 solar panels.

Across the continent, more and more areas are becoming **ANTARCTIC SPECIALLY PROTECTED AREAS**, or ASPAs. This means that they are managed by groups of people who ensure that the landscape and wildlife remain as undisturbed as possible.

GLOSSARY

adaptation The process in which a living thing changes slightly over time to be able to continue to exist in a particular environment.

albedo effect The way in which dark colours absorb (soak up) heat, and light colours reflect it.

algae Tiny plant-like organisms that live in polar regions. Algae are food for the animals that live there.

anti-freeze A substance used to lower the freezing point of water.

axis An imaginary line drawn through the middle of the Earth, between the North and South Poles.

carbon dioxide A gas found in the atmosphere. It is released when fuel, such as coal or wood, burns and when animals breathe out.

climate The usual pattern of weather that happens in a place.

climate change Changes in the world's weather patterns caused by human activity, such as burning fossil fuels.

crustacean A type of animal that lives in water and has a hard outer shell.

ecosystem A community of animals and plants and the habitat they live in.

fluke The lobe of a whale's tail.

food web The way in which living things are linked together by what they eat.

fossil fuels Fuels made from the remains of dead animals and plants that lived millions of years ago.

generator A machine that often runs on petrol and produces electricity.

greenhouse gases Gases that trap heat in the atmosphere.

habitat A place or type of surroundings where living things are usually found.

incubate When a bird keeps its eggs warm until the chicks are ready to hatch.

invertebrates Animals that do not have backbones or skeletons inside their bodies.

krill Tiny shrimp-like animals that live in the ocean and provide food for other sea creatures.

lab (short for laboratory) A building or room set up for scientific research.

migrate To move from one place to another according to the seasons.

overwintering To spend the winter in a place.

pigment A substance that colours something.

pollution When air, soil or water are spoiled or made dirty or harmful by something else.

windchill factor The way in which the wind makes it feel colder than it actually is. The stronger the wind, the colder it feels.

zero-emissions When something doesn't release any gases, such as carbon dioxide, into the air.

FURTHER INFO

Books:

Blue Worlds: The Southern Ocean by Anita Ganeri and Josy Bloggs

Continents Uncovered: Australia, New Zealand and Antarctica by Rob Colson (Franklin Watts, 2024)

Wildlife Worlds: Australasia and Antarctica by Tim Harris (Wayland, 2020)

Websites:

http://www.antarcticstation.org/station

This is the webpage of the Princess Elizabeth research station that gives some insight into all the zero-emissions technology used at the facility.

www.youtube.com/watch?v=dgPqyCvjDxg

A short film about life on Halley VI by the British Antarctic Survey

www.youtube.com/watch?v=t57DPnH06V0

Some beautiful footage of the Antarctic winter sky with aurora

We strongly advise that Internet access is supervised by a responsible adult. The website addresses (URLs) included in this book were valid at the time of going to press. However, it is possible that contents or addresses may have changed since the publication of this book. No responsibility for any such changes can be accepted by either the author or the Publisher.

INDEX

algae 25
Amundsen, Roald 35
Antarctic Treaty 37
Arctic 4, 32
aurore australis 16-17
autumn 25, 31

birds 11, 14, 21, 23, 25, 29-33
  Arctic tern 32
  penguins *see separate entry*
  southern skuas 33
  wandering albatross 33
climate 4, 6-8, 15-16, 20-21, 39, 42
climate change 36, 42
crystals, ice 18-19

Davis, John 34
dust, diamond 18-19

effect, albedo 6
explorers 35

fish 12-13, 23, 27-29, 33
floes, ice 11
food web, Antarctic 20, 22-23

glaciers 9, 43

ice 4, 6-9, 11, 14, 20, 24, 30-31, 37-40, 43
  ice sheets 9, 25, 39, 43
  ice shelves 9, 39, 43
pack ice 11, 13, 29, 35
sea ice 10-11, 14, 20-21, 28-29, 43
icebergs 9
invertebrates 12-13, 25
  glyptonotus 12

krill 13, 22, 26-27

lichen 24

Mount Erebus 7
mosses 25

penguins 11, 14, 21, 23, 25, 29-31, 43
phytoplankton 20, 22
plankton 22
plants 7, 20, 24-25
Pole, North 4, 17
Pole, South 5-6, 14, 17, 35, 39
pollution 40-41, 43, 45

research stations 38-39
  Halley VI 39
  Princess Elizabeth research station 45
  Rothera research station 39

scientists 22, 25, 33, 36, 38-40, 45
sealers 34
seals 14, 21-23, 28-29, 34
Shackleton, Ernest 35
snow 4, 7-8, 25, 38
southern lights 16-17
spring 11, 20-21, 25
squid 23, 27-29, 33
summer 10, 18, 25-26, 28-29, 32-33, 36-37, 41

tourism 36-37

weather 4, 7, 11, 14-15, 18, 31, 39, 42
Weddell, James 34
whales 21-22, 26-27, 34
winter 14-15, 20, 26, 28-33